Nelson Mandela

Ambujam Anantharaman

Nelson Mandela

First Edition: March 2009

64 Pages

Printed in India.

ISBN 978–81–8493–094–8

Pro–ya–en–36

Prodigy Books is an imprint of
New Horizon Media Pvt. Ltd.
177/103, First Floor,
Ambal's Building, Lloyds Road,
Royapettah, Chennai 600 014.
Ph: +91-44-4200-9603

Email: support@nhm.in
Website: www.nhm.in

Introduction

If you go to South Africa today, you can travel in the same bus or train as a white person, sit at the same dining table with them in a restaurant and live wherever you want in that beautiful country. For much of the 20th century, this was not the case. There existed a policy which separated people based on the colour of their skins. For example, Africans had to live in an Africans-Only area, attend Africans-Only schools, seek medical help in an Africans-Only hospital, travel only in Africans-Only buses and trains and hold Africans-Only jobs. This policy of racial discrimination, which made the white man superior to Africans, coloured people and Indians too, was called apartheid. The word apartheid literally means 'apart'.

Africans were treated as second-class people. We cannot even use the word citizens, because they did not have the right to vote in an election. Very early in the last century, in 1912 to be precise, an organization called the ANC was formed to get equal rights and liberation for Africans living in South Africa. There was a long struggle to achieve this and only in 1994, Africans voted for the first time to form a government of their own choice.

The ANC came to power after the election, and its leader Nelson Mandela was sworn in as the first African president of South Africa. It was the country's first democratic, non-racial government and as Mandela was sworn in on 10 May 1994, he said in his speech 'Today all of us do by our presence here.... confer glory and hope to newborn liberty. Out of the experience of an extra-ordinary human disaster that lasted too long must be born a society of which, all humanity will be proud. Never and never again shall it be that this beautiful land will again experience the oppression of one by another... the sun shall never set on so glorious a human achievement. Let freedom reign, God Bless Africa.'

In the true spirit of equality, along with Mandela, F W de Klerk, the leader of the Nationalist Party, a white man who played a large role in shifting power to the majority Africans, was sworn in as Second Deputy President. His Nationalist party had lost the elections, but Mandela stayed true to his promise to give representation to all–black and white–in the government.

Thabo Mbeki, who became the South African President after Mandela retired due to old age, was sworn in as the First Deputy President that day in 1994. In the colourful function, jets left a smoke trail of black, red, green, blue and gold–colours of the new South African flag. Two national anthems were played, that of the Whites and that of the Africans. The generals of the South African Defence Forces and the Police saluted Mandela and pledged their loyalty to him when in the past, they would have arrested him. What a transformation the man and his comrades had achieved through unimaginable sacrifices, suffering and courage!

As hundreds of international visitors watched, a new South Africa was born. Let us recount the story of the man, Nelson Mandela and how he became the Father of the South African Nation.

Childhood

Let us begin at the very beginning of the African's struggle for equality in South Africa–the birth of Nelson Mandela, and trace his life and his achievements. We will start with his childhood.

A boy was born on 18 July 1918 in a small village called Mvezo. He was named Rolihlahla though he was supposed to be called Nelson in school. Located on the banks of the Mbeashe River in the Umtata District, the region was called the Transkei. Transkei lies eight hundred miles east of Cape Town and five hundred and fifty miles south of Johannesburg. In his autobiography, "Long Road to Freedom", Mandela calls it 'a beautiful country of rolling hills, fertile valleys and a thousand rivers and streams, which keep the landscape green even in winter.'

It had a population of three and a half million Xhosas who are one of South Africa's main communities. It is the home of the Thembu people, of whom Mandela is part. Every Xhosa belongs to a clan, and Mandela was a member of the Madiba clan, named after a Thembu chief who ruled in the 18th century. Even today he is often addressed as Madiba, a term of respect.

Mandela's father Gadla Henry Mphakanyiswa was a Chief by inheritance. As per the laws of the day, his chiefdom had to be approved by the government and in his position as Chief he was paid a stipend, compensation, by the government. Mandela's father was an advisor to the rulers of the tribe.

In his early years Mandela was brought up in the house of the Regent to the ruler Sabata. A Regent is someone who looks after the administration of a region till the rightful ruler is old enough to take over. The Regent's name was Jonjintaba, and he was the son of Sabata's father by a different wife. Jonjintaba had great regard for Mandela's father because it was he who recommended that Jonjintaba and not one of his brothers should be appointed Regent. We must note here that it was the custom in the tribe to have several wives. Mandela's father had four wives and thirteen children and Mandela's mother Nosekeni Fanny was his third wife. She had her own Kraal, which is a homestead that consists of an enclosure for animals, thatched huts and fields for growing crops .

When Mandela was very young, his father lost his Chieftainship. His father believed that he should report only to the Thembu king and no one else, and therefore he refused to appear before the local magistrate who summoned him in connection with a minor complaint against him involving an ox that had strayed from its owner. The magistrate charged him with insubordination for refusing to appear and dismissed him. The result was that Mandela's father lost not only his title, but his income too. Owing to the difficult circumstances, his mother moved to Qunu, a somewhat bigger village, north of Mvezo, where she had friends and relatives. As a result, Mandela spent his childhood and his boyhood in Qunu.

Qunu had a population of a few hundred, all of whom lived in huts. The women and children wore blankets, which was the traditional attire of the tribe. It was a life moulded by custom, ritual and taboo. Straying from these was strictly condemned. They worshipped the great spirit of the Xhosas, called Qamata. Mandela's mother however became a Christian and Nelson was baptized into the Methodist church.

Mandela's mother had three huts. One was used for cooking, one for sleeping and the third for storage. The family slept on a mat and sat on the ground. They planted and harvested their own Mealies (Maize). They got milk from their cows and goats. It is important to remember that during Mandela's childhood, the land belonged to the state and not to the inhabitants as per rules. Apart from a few exceptions, Africans at that time could not own any land! Qunu had two small primary schools, a general store and a tank for livestock. The crops grown were Maize, which was called Mealies, Sorghum, Beans and Pumpkins. The richer families in the village had Tea, Coffee and Sugar. There were few men in the village because they either worked in far away farms or in the mines near Johannesburg. Mandela came across few whites as a boy–the local magistrate and a couple of others. He learnt very soon that they were treated with a mix of fear and respect by the Africans.

From a young age, Mandela spent his time playing and fighting with other boys of the village. He was just five when he became a shepherd who looked after sheep and calves in the fields. Mandela and his fellow herders enjoyed themselves in the fields played games, gathered wild honey and fruits, drank warm fresh milk and swam in the streams. Mandela learnt to fight with a stick, which was one of the common pursuits. Sometimes, the girls would join the boys. Mandela's father would tell stories of historic battles and brave Xhosa warriors during his visits to Qunu, while his mother would tell Xhosa legends and fables. These tales fired the child's imagination. Under the influence of his father's friends, George and Ben Mbekela, the young Nelson was sent to school.

Student Days

The day before he was to begin school, which was quite near his home, Mandela's father told him he had to be dressed suitably and could not wear a blanket. He took a pair of his own trousers, cut them at the knee and tied them round the boy's waist with a piece of string. It was also on the first day of school that his teacher, Miss Mdeingana, gave him an English name, Nelson.

Two years later, Mandela's father died. His mother told him that he was leaving Qunu but did not tell him where he was going. They walked till they came to a large house–the likes of which Mandela had never seen before. It was the royal home of Chief Jonjintaba, Regent of the Thembu people. Jonjintaba had offered to become Mandela's guardian and his mother had accepted. While living under the Regent's care, Mandela attended a one-room school neighbouring the palace. He studied English, Xhosa, History and Geography and was a good student. His companions were Jongintaba's children, Justice, the heir, and Nomafu, his sister. He was treated in the same way that the Regent's children were, and Justice and Mandela became close friends.

Mandela heard of many African heroes during his stay at the Regent's house and became interested in African history. He also became accustomed to attending church every Sunday, something he didn't do in his hometown. He states that observing the Regent and his court profoundly influenced his later notions of leadership. Very often in the tribal meetings held there, those who attended the meetings criticized the Regent who never objected. As Mandela says in his autobiography 'I always remember the Regent's axiom: a leader, he said, is like a shepherd. He stays behind the flock letting the most nimble go out ahead, whereupon the others follow, not realizing that all along, they are being directed from behind.'

After a ceremony there were speeches by many leaders. One such speech was by Chief Meligquili. He remarked 'We Xhosas and all black South Africans are a conquered people. We are slaves in our own country.' This was what first made Mandela aware that he and people like him were very different from the few white men he had happened to encounter.

When he turned sixteen, he was sent to study in Clarkbury Boarding Institute, about sixty miles from the Regent's house. It was one of the well-regarded educational institutions for Africans in Thembu. It was a secondary school as well as a teacher training college and also taught carpentry, tailoring and other vocations. Here, Mandela learnt English, History and other subjects The Governor of the school was one Reverend C Harris, who was a white man who loved the Thembu people. While working in the Reverend's garden, Mandela developed a love of gardening, which would stand him in good stead later in his life, when he was imprisoned for many years.

In 1937, at the age of nineteen, he joined Justice at Healdtown, a Wesleyan college located in Fort Beaufort. He then graduated to the University College of Fort Hare, the sole residential centre of higher education for blacks in South Africa. He studied English, Anthropology, Politics, Native Administration and Roman Dutch Law among other subjects and aimed towards getting a B.A. degree. However he did not complete his studies in this college.

The incidents which led to the abrupt end of Mandela's studies reflect several important features of his character–his strong principles and his ability to sacrifice anything for his beliefs. Elections were to be held for the posts of office bearers in the Students Representative Council and Mandela was among those who were running for the post. However the students decided to boycott the elections and demanded better food and living conditions. When the elections were held, only 25 students voted and 6 students, including Mandela, were elected to the Council. All six resigned. On the next day, the authorities held the election in the dining room with all students present. Once again only 25 voted, but 5 of the elected decided not to resign, as they thought this was a fair way of getting elected. Mandela differed and chose to resign, following which he was expelled from the college. He later completed his B.A. degree by correspondence.

Mandela went back home. To his shock, the Regent told him that he and Justice were to be married shortly. Both of them were so upset at the news that they ran away to Johannesburg!

Career as a Lawyer

Mandela was now in Johannesburg, having left his University and run away from home. After an unsuccessful attempt to work at the mines, Mandela went to stay with a relative, who took him to meet a real-estate agent for help. This agent was none other than Walter Sisulu, who was to become Mandela's close associate in the long struggle for African rights. Sisulu introduced him to a white lawyer named Lazar Sidelsky, who took Mandela on as a clerk.

At the end of 1942, Mandela passed the final examination for his B.A. degree and graduated. Early the next year, he enrolled at the University of Witwatersrand for a Bachelors of Law degree. He became a full-time student after completing his apprenticeship at the firm of *Witkin, Sidelsky and Eidelman*. It was during his time at this firm that Mandela got exposed to the ANC–the pioneer in campaigning for equal rights for Africans in South Africa. He later became one of the most prominent leaders of this organization.

After completing his articleship, Mandela went to work for the law firm *Terblanche and Briggish* and later for *Helman and Michel.* There were only white law firms and no African law firms at that time. These white firms charged Africans a higher fee than they charged their white clients. *Helman and Michel* did not do this, and so Mandela stayed with them for a number of months while he studied for his qualification examination. When he passed the exam, he joined the firm *H.M Basner* as a full-fledged attorney. Bassner was a passionate supporter of African Rights.

In August 1953 Mandela opened his own law office, along with another ANC activist, Oliver Tambo, who was later to become President of the ANC. They took up many cases on behalf of African and coloured people. These included several cases involving police brutality. They often did not succeed in these cases because the magistrates invariably supported the police, but that did not stop them from trying repeatedly.

Throughout his career as a lawyer, Mandela made every effort to improve the conditions and protect the rights of his fellow African people. As a member of the ANC, he was an active member of the political movement to get equal rights for Africans. Due to his political activities, the Law Society of the Transvaal applied to the Supreme Court for his name to be struck off the rolls of attorneys in April 1954. Mandela won the case because his advocate told the court of the case of a white man who had practiced as an advocate, despite his being politically active.

Mandela's law firm had to close when he was arrested, which we shall describe later. After his return from prison, he continued to do legal work using the offices of friends and colleagues.

The African National Congress

The ANC was the oldest national African organization in the country and had been founded as early as 1912. Its goal was to make Africans full citizens of South Africa and it spearheaded a long and hard liberation struggle. This struggle was against the apartheid policy, which did not give Africans the right to vote in the country's election.

Mandela's senior in the law firm of *Witkin, Sidelsky and Eidelman* was Gaur Radebe, a man who was totally committed to the freedom struggle. It was with him that Mandela first went to meetings of the ANC. Walter Sisulu's house was the place where ANC activists gathered to talk. ANC members included not only Africans, but also Indians and coloured people, making it a broad-based organization. Initially, Mandela was only an observer in ANC meetings. He never used to speak in the lively meetings, which used to discuss the parliament, the rule that Africans should have passes, rents and bus fares. For the first time along with Radebe and 10,000 others, Mandela marched in support of a bus boycott protesting the sudden bus fare hike.

From this time, Mandela's life was intimately involved with the activities of the ANC. His experiences at University and as a lawyer had made him acutely conscious of the fact that he was a black and he soon realized that he would be a committed participant in the liberation struggle. Let us now look at the evolution of this organization and the pivotal part Mandela played in it.

In the 1940s, activism against apartheid picked up and the ANC created a charter called African Claims, calling for full citizenship for all Africans. In order to increase its influence and bring more Africans into the liberation struggle, in 1944, the ANC Youth League was formed to recruit new members. Its battle cry was African Nationalism. Its manifesto opposed anti-African legislation such as

> the Land Act, which deprived coloured people 87% of the South African territory,

the Urban Areas Act, which created highly populated African slums,

the Colour Bar Act, which banned Africans from practicing skilled trades,

the Native Administration Act, which made the British Crown chief of all African areas,

the Representation of Natives Act, which deprived Africans voting powers.

1946 was another hallmark year during which 70,000 African miners went on strike for better minimum wages among other demands. The government acted immediately and arrested the leaders of the strike. Police attacked during a march and 12 miners died. This strike had a deep impact on Mandela's mind, as did a new law, which curtailed Indian rights. The Indians protested through a mass campaign that became a model for the type of protests the Youth League later undertook.

In 1947, Mandela got his first position in the ANC. He was elected to the Executive Committee of the Transvaal ANC. The same year, a pact was signed uniting different organizations like the ANC, the Transvaal Indian Congress, the Natal Indian Congress, and later, the African Peoples Organization.

With regard to his personal life, Mandela had married Evelyn Mase, whom he had met in Walter Sisulu's house during ANC meetings. They had two sons and two daughters. Mandela was so involved with the movement that he hardly spent any time at home, so much so that his elder son once asked Evelyn, 'Where does Daddy live?'

The situation for Africans worsened in 1948, during the general elections in South Africa. The United Party, led by Jan Smuts lost, and the National Party, a party of Afrikaaners won. The Nationalists slogan was 'White man must always remain boss'. The Nationalists introduced more laws, which were anti-African. For example, the government forced Africans to move out of their homes in Johannesburg to a new settlement. In yet another move, the government took over African education, openly stating that Africans would be educated only up to a certain level so that the Africans would not become well educated.

The ANC, aware that it had to keep active to counter these moves, implemented a Program of Action, calling for boycotts, strikes, stay-at-homes, passive resistance and protest demonstrations. This mass action was planned along the lines of Mahatma Gandhi's non-violent struggle in India. To protest against the oppressive laws introduced by the government, a one-day general strike was planned and this took place on 1 May 1950, when over two-thirds of the African workers stayed at home. Inevitably, the police attacked the march held on the occasion and 18 Africans died. This outrage prompted the ANC to call a National Day of Protest on 26 June. This day, 26 June, became a landmark day in the freedom struggle and it came to be known as Freedom Day.

The activism next found expression in a National Civil Disobedience campaign. This was to be held in two stages. In the first, volunteers would break laws and use facilities meant only for whites and get arrested. The second stage would be mass defiance with strikes and industrial action across the country. Mandela was President of the Youth League when the National Civil Disobedience campaign was launched on 26 June 1952, the anniversary of the first National Day of Protest. Mandela went to prison for the first time after participating in the campaign, along with 250 other volunteers. Over the next five months, 8500 people-doctors, lawyers, teachers, ministers, factory workers, students took part in the campaign and went to jail. The campaign gave the ANC a popularity and public support and membership increased from 20,000 to

100,000. Mandela went around the country organizing the campaign.

The Government banned him from attending any meeting and from moving out of the district of Johannesburg. He couldn't even attend his son's birthday party. Mandela sensed that the ANC itself would soon be banned, just like the communist party had been. So, he suggested setting up of proper organizational machinery for the ANC so that it could function even if it was banned.

The next significant year is 1955, when a Congress of the People was held, and 3,000 delegates attended braving police threats. The meeting passed a very important document called Freedom Charter, which became a mark of the liberation struggle. Importantly the Charter stated that South Africa belonged to all who lived in it, both black and white. It did not say that the country belonged only to Africans. When his ban expired, Mandela went all over South Africa–to Durban, Port Elizabeth and Cape Town–to meet people and to get to know the ground realities there.

The Treason Trial

There was a loud knocking on the door of Mandela's house, early in the morning on December 5, 1956. Mandela immediately knew that only the police would knock like that. Indeed it was the police who entered the house and searched it. Mandela's children were frightened. They arrested him on a charge of high treason. Treason means betrayal, in this case it was against the government.

When Mandela reached prison, he found that a number of his colleagues in the ANC, especially its leaders, were already there. The prisoners were lodged in cells with very poor facilities. The only plus factor was that all of them were together in two cells, and not in individual cells. This kept their spirits up. They were charged with a countrywide conspiracy to use violence to overthrow the government. The state's case against the prisoners was 18,000 words long! As the prisoners were taken to court and the charges against them read, large crowds of supporters thronged the court to express their solidarity with Mandela and others. The defence team had many eminent lawyers and well-wishers who started a Treason Trial Defence Fund to pay the bail for those arrested.

Meanwhile, Mandela's personal life was troubled, as his wife did not like his political activism. They finally separated.

Out on bail, Mandela continued his legal work during the day, while his evenings were spent with ANC people. On 9 January 1957, the legal proceedings started again and the defence lawyers stated the government's charges were false and pleaded not guilty. The actual trial was yet to begin and already several months had passed. It was during this time that Mandela met his second wife Winnie, who would participate actively in the freedom struggle for many years. They got married in 1958, and since Mandela was unable to continue practicing law, they lived on Winnie's small salary as a social worker.

As the months drew on, the State decided to withdraw the charges as the case was not prepared well, but soon launched fresh charges. In the midst of all this, Mandela became a father again. Winnie had a girl child.

On the political front, another African organization was started. It was called the Pan Africanist Congress. It differed from the ANC in that it refused to include groups like the Indians. Mandela felt that the formation of the PAC divided the African people. Meanwhile the Government continued its apartheid policies. It created separate tribal homelands, meaning each tribe was restricted to a specific area. In other words, 70% of the people were given just 13% of the land. The people protested and there was a fresh round of arrests, beatings and murders.

Going back to the treason trial, 2 years and 8 months after the arrests, on 3rd August 1959, the actual trial began. As the treason trial was proceeding, the PAC launched a campaign against Africans having to carry passes. On 21 March, 1960, a major tragedy occurred which people in South Africa still remember. In the small township of Sharpsville, about 35 miles from Johannesburg, a crowd of several thousand people surrounded the police station. They were unarmed. The police suddenly opened fire and sixty-nine Africans were killed, most of them shot in the back as they were running away. Many international agencies like the

American State Department and the UN Security Council condemned the shootings. The situation in South Africa changed overnight. The ANC responded by publicly burning the passes of its members and 100,000 Africans observed a stay-at-home and a national day of mourning.

The Government declared a state of emergency and assumed sweeping powers. Immediately after this, Mandela and many of his colleagues in the ANC were rearrested under the Emergency regulations. They were all put in a tiny cell with virtually no drainage; they were given no blankets, no food and no mats. When they protested against the conditions they were given blankets that were too filthy to be used. Over two thousand people were detained without trial, they belonged to all races and all anti-apartheid parties. On 8 April, both the ANC and PAC were declared illegal organizations.

Meanwhile in the rest of Africa, 17 colonies became independent states raising hopes in South Africa. The treason trial continued with the accused attending every day from prison and returning to prison after the session was over. Just before emergency had been declared the ANC took a major step, which would help it greatly. Oliver Tambo, one of its foremost activists, left South Africa to live outside and carry on its work. Mandela was given special permission to visit his law office on weekends with the aim of putting things in order to close the practice. He met Winnie on his visits to the law office. During this time, Winnie gave birth to another daughter.

Mandela, in his testimony from 3 August used the platform to voice their demands and to reaffirm the ANC's commitment to a non-violent struggle. The prosecution tried its best to prove that he was a dangerous, violence-spouting communist.

The judges gave a verdict favourable to the ANC. To the cheering from the spectators' gallery, they announced that the accused had been found not guilty and that they would be discharged. So ended the treason trial, after four long years!

The Black Pimpernel

The Scarlet Pimpernel is a character in a novel who escapes during the French Revolution by moving from place to place. Mandela, who did the same, was named the Black Pimpernel.

After the verdict in the treason trial, Mandela did not return home. Instead he began travelling to several parts of South Africa, spreading the message of the ANC. After spending the night in a safe house in Johannesburg, he began the first leg of his journey to Port Elizabeth. At different safe houses, he and other ANC members discussed the new underground structures of the organization. They also talked about a campaign for a national convention. Mandela then quickly moved to Cape Town where he engaged in similar activities. He then went to Durban where a secret meeting of the ANC National Executive Committee was held. This meeting decided on calling for yet another 'stay-at-home'. Mandela said, 'living underground required a psychological shift'. He had to plan every small action and could not be himself. He became a creature of the night. He would stay in a hideout during the day and do his work after dark. He lived in empty flats, in people's houses, wherever he could. He literally became invisible. He disguised himself as a chauffeur, a chef, a garden-boy or a field worker. There was a warrant for his arrest and the police was pursuing him. His secret existence caught the imagination of the press, which published articles claiming that he had been seen in some place or the other. The police would immediately set up roadblocks but was unable to arrest him.

There were several narrow escapes. Once, when he was travelling by car, he stopped at a traffic light. He looked to his left and to his shock saw a senior police officer in the car right next to him. Fortunately for him, the officer never looked to his right. On another occasion, when he was in Johannesburg, he was standing at a corner, waiting to be picked up by a friend. He saw an African policeman striding towards him and thought it was all over. To his pleasant surprise, the policeman smiled at him, surreptitiously gave him the thumbs up ANC salute and passed by. This secret life had humorous moments as well. Once, a priest and his friends arranged to put Mandela up for the night. When Mandela knocked on the door, it was opened by an elderly lady, who on seeing his bearded and unkempt appearance, exclaimed 'No we don't want a man like you here!' and shut the door on his face. She had obviously not recognized him.

As we said earlier, a stay-at-home agitation was planned on 29 May 1961. The government responded with strict measures. It organized countrywide raids on opposition leaders, banned meetings, seized printing presses and passed legislation permitting police to detain prisoners for 12 days without bail. In a show of force, it stationed military units at the entrances and exits of townships, drove tanks through streets, used helicopters to swoop down on any gathering and to train searchlights on houses. The stay-at-home was a big success, with hundreds of thousands of people not going to work.

The Government's measures prompted Mandela to feel that the days of the non-violent struggle were over and new tactics had to be adopted. After several meetings with ANC leaders and leaders of friendly organizations, his ideas were finally accepted. He was put in charge of starting a new organization called Umkhonto we Sizwe.

Translated, it means 'The Spear of the Nation'. The organization was called MK for short.

Mandela stayed underground and began working towards the success of MK. The strategy was to hit military installations, power plants, telephone lines and transportation links. For example, members were trained to set off explosions. The MK held meetings at a place called Liliesleaf Farm discussed four types of violent activity - sabotage, guerrilla warfare, terrorism and open revolution. They put the last three aside and decided to concentrate on sabotage, which would cause the least harm to the people. Homemade bombs were exploded at electric power stations and government offices in Johannesburg, Port Elizabeth and Durban on December 16, 1961. Another set of explosions was set off on New Year's Eve. Thousands of leaflets with the MK manifesto were distributed all over the country.

After a series of short-term homes, Mandela moved to Liliesleaf Farm, located in Rivonia, a northern suburb of Johannesburg. He changed his name to David Motsamayi and dressed in simple blue overalls, worked as a caretaker. Mandela's family visited him at the farm, much to his happiness.

Visit abroad to get support

In December the same year, the ANC got an invitation from the Pan-African Freedom Movement for East, Central and Southern Africa (PAFMECSA) to attend its conference in Addis Ababa in February 1962. PAFMECSA, which later became the Organization of African Unity, was seen by the ANC as a wonderful opportunity to get important connections and enlist support for MK.

The ANC asked Mandela to attend the conference. The aim was not only to get political and economic support for ANC's new military force, but to also obtain military training for the cadre in as many places on the African continent as possible. To go to Addis Ababa, Mandela had to first travel to Dar-es-Salaam in Tanganyika.

Mandela drove to a place called Lobatse, quite near the South African border. He passed through the border without a problem and landed in Lobatse, which was located in Bechuanaland. He and a couple of others who accompanied him chartered a plane and reached Tanganyika.

To Mandela's astonishment, he saw a crowd of blacks and whites sitting and chatting on the veranda of the hotel he was staying in. He had never been in a public place where there was no colour bar. In the capital Dar-es-Salaam, Mandela met the newly independent country's first President, Julius Nyerere. Mandela appealed to him for help. After passing through Khartoum, Mandela boarded a flight to Ethiopia. He was stunned to see that the pilot was a black man.

Ethiopia was considered the birthplace of African nationalism. Again Mandela had a surprise, when he witnessed a parade before the Emperor of Ethiopia Haile Sclassie. 'Here for the first time in my life, I was witnessing black soldiers, commanded by black generals, applauded by black leaders who are all guests of a black head of state... I only hoped it was a vision of what lay in the future of my own country.' After the parade, the conference began and Mandela spoke immediately after the Emperor. He described the history of the freedom struggle in South Africa and talked of the brutal massacres committed against the Africans. He thanked the countries of Ghana, Nigeria and Tanganyka, which had helped successfully remove South Africa from the British Commonwealth. He also spoke of the MK and explained why it had been launched.

From Ethiopia, Mandela flew to Egypt and then to Tunisia, Morocco, Algeria, Mali, Guinea, Sierra Leone, Liberia, Ghana and Senegal. Mandela then went to London and moved around secretly there, not wanting the South African authorities to know where he was. Wherever he went, he explained the goal of the ANC to the people he met, and sought help not only in the form of support, but also in money and military training. After his visit to London, he went back to Addis Ababa for six months of military training. He learnt how to shoot a pistol, an automatic rifle, how to make small bombs and mines and about demolition and mortar firing. In theory lectures he was taught how to create a guerrilla force and how to command an army.

The training was cut short at 8 weeks when he received a telegram from the ANC urgently asking him to return home. The internal armed struggle was heightening and the commander of MK had to be on the spot. Carrying several thousand pounds of currency notes given to him by various well-wishers, he reached South Africa by way of Khartoum and Dar-es-Salaam.

Long years in jail

Soon after Mandela returned from his African trip, he was arrested in 1962 while driving from Durban to Johannesburg. He was put in a cell by himself but soon realized that nearby, in another cell, was Walter Sisulu. Mandela was charged for leaving the country without valid travel documents and for inciting African workers to strike. The papers carried headline news: 'Police swoop ends two years on the run'. Mandela was personally relieved that he had not been arrested for his MK activities.

The ANC set up a 'Free Mandela' committee and launched a campaign. Mandela spoke for himself in court and described the case as 'a trial of the aspirations of the African people'. However, he did not defend himself as he saw that the state had a solid case. The magistrate awarded a sentence of five years in jail and he was put in solitary confinement. After several protests at this treatment, he was put in a section that housed other political prisoners.

Meanwhile, there was good news from outside South Africa during the trial. The UN General Assembly voted in favour of sanctions against South Africa for the first time. Acts of sabotage within the nation also continued.

In 1963, South Africa virtually became a police state after a law was passed stating that any police officer could detain a person without warrant and the person could be held without trial, charge or access to a lawyer for 90 days. The police also took advantage of the situation and allegedly indulged in torture of prisoners. Towards the end of May 1963, Mandela was transferred to a prison called 'The Island'. This was the infamous Robben Island, located off Cape Town, which had the reputation of being one of the toughest jails.

As he entered the prison, he was met by a group of white warders shouting 'This is the Island, here you will die!' He immediately resisted by disobeying their order to walk fast. Mandela and his fellow prisoners had a very tough life in the prison. They had to do manual labour every day.

One day, he was taken back to a prison in Pretoria on the pretext that his life was in danger from other prisoners in Robben Island. In July 1963, he was summoned to the prison office and saw that several of his ANC colleagues and MK members were there. He realized that their secret retreat, the Liliesleaf farm had been discovered. All of them had been charged with two hundred acts of sabotage based on the documents and papers seized by the police from the farm. Other charges included planning a violent revolution and the armed invasion of the country by foreign powers. The State contended that the prisoners were conspiring to overthrow the government. The penalty was death by hanging.

By this time, the police was following Winnie Mandela, and her house was searched repeatedly. Mandela was disturbed to find that his wife could not come to the court. She too had been banned from leaving Johannesburg. Later she got permission to attend the trial.

The state had with it a plan of action for guerrilla operations seized from the farm. In actual fact, the plan had not yet been adopted and was still under discussion. Mandela addressed the court again, stressing that fifty years of non-violence had brought the African people nothing and that they had made preparations to use force in order to defend themselves against the state which used force. He also described 'the terrible disparities between black and white lives in South Africa'. His address took four hours.

The main accused were found guilty of all the charges by the judge on 11 June, 1964. The next day, they were all sentenced to life imprisonment as the judge had decided against imposing the death penalty. Mandela felt that international pressure and the demonstrations throughout South Africa had influenced the judge. Soon, it was back to Robben Island for 46-year old Mandela.

Life in Robben Island was dreary and strenuous. Mandela's cell was so small that when he lay down, he could feel the wall with his feet and his head grazed the concrete on the other end. It was terribly cold and they were given just a mat to lie on. African prisoners had to wear short trousers–a strange regulation that allowed Indian prisoners, for example, to wear long trousers.

Every morning they were woken up at 5:30 and had to clean their cells till they were let out at 6:45 am. There was no running water in the cells and instead of toilets, there were given iron sanitary buckets known as 'Ballies'.

The first chore of the morning, after leaving the cell, was to clean the Ballies. Since the warders did not like to stay while the cleaning was being done, it was an opportunity for the prisoners to have a few whispered words with one another. Breakfast consisted of Mealies porridge. After breakfast, the prisoners had to stand outside their cells for inspection. Each prisoner had to have the three buttons of his khaki jacket buttoned. They had to salute the warder by removing their hats as he walked by. After inspection, they had to work in the courtyard hammering stones into small pieces. Strangely, when visitors came, the prisoners would be given easier work like stitching. As they hammered the stones, flying chips caused injuries. Lunch was Mealies again, and so was dinner. As the kitchen was full of smuggling, they got less than the already meagre allotment. The food was delivered by the common prisoners. Common prisoners were a different group from political prisoners like Mandela and were in jail for various crimes like theft. In another strange discriminatory practice, other coloured and Indian prisoners would get bread and margarine. Africans did not, because it was claimed that they would not care for 'European type of food'. Work would get over at four, after which they were given half an hour to clean up.

At 8 pm, the night warder would lock himself in the corridor with the prisoners and pass the key out. He would then order them to go to sleep. The single bulb in each cell burned day and night, so there was no question of total darkness. Many visitors, some of them journalists, would visit the prison, because of the concern outside about the conditions and their treatment. The political prisoners, who had the strictest rules and restrictions among all the prisoners, used to nominate Mandela to speak on their behalf. He would talk about the problems they faced, but there was rarely any improvement.

The prisoners used to look forward to letters eagerly. Often the warders would not hand over a letter, meant for a prisoner, but would spitefully tell him that he had received a letter. The letters were censored by cutting out portions that might upset the prisoner in anyway, and hence, they would be received in tatters. Visits were few and far between because the families of most of the prisoners lived far away. Wives of prisoners would be contacted and told 'you have permission to visit your husband tomorrow'. The wife could hardly make such a long distance at such short notice and some prisoners did not see their wives for many years at a time. Winnie Mandela did visit Nelson, but they were separated from each other by thick glass. The glass had a few holes drilled into it for the prisoner and the visitor to talk, and the visit only lasted for a maximum of half an hour. The warders would be present during the talk to assess if anything political was being discussed. Winnie was in great difficulties at this point of time because she had been terminated from her job at a child welfare office, following a ban.

In January 1965, the manual labour became much more difficult. They were taken to a quarry every day to mine lime. This gave the prisoners blisters and their hands used to bleed. The only advantage was that being outside the prison they could see grass and trees, watch birds fly and feel the wind. The warders, armed with automatic weapons would shout at the prisoners to work harder. As the sun rose, the prisoners would begin to tire but the warders would drive them even harder. Their problems were made worse because the glare from the sun hurt their eyes. They pleaded for sunglasses and after three years, they were given them. Mandela, being an attorney, would write to the authorities if some atrocity happened like a prisoner being beaten or tortured.

In the summer of 1965, the food suddenly improved and they got fresh meat. Some of the prisoners also got new shirts. In prison, no improvement happened without a reason, said Mandela. As expected, there were to be important visitors–namely, the International Red Cross. Mandela was called to meet the Red Cross representative and he voiced all the complaints and grievances the prisoners had. After this, some of the conditions did improve. The Red Cross also provided money to wives and relatives who would have not been able to visit the Island otherwise. Another improvement came when the prisoners were given permission to study. Subjects like politics and military history were prohibited, but others were permitted. Mandela studied under the sponsorship of the University of London. Receiving books was very difficult, particularly because the censors had to check them. After the Red Cross intervened, the authorities built a stand up desk–a simple wooden board in each cell.

Getting information and news from the outside world was one of the biggest challenges in prison. Prisoners in the general section were more aware of what was happening in the outside world because there was greater inflow and outflow among them. The political prisoners devised several ingenious ways to communicate with the general prisoners. One was to write messages and place them in a false bottom of matchboxes. Another was to put letters and notes wrapped in plastic at the bottom of the food drums. Plastic wrapped notes would even be taped inside the rim of the toilet bowl. A sure fire method was to give letters to visiting lawyers, since lawyers were not searched. They would also use coded language with visitors. For example Mandela asked his wife during her second visit to the prison, which came two years after the first, how the church was. Church here meant the ANC.

In another tactic, the warder's sandwiches used to be wrapped in newspaper, which they would throw aside in the garbage. The prisoners would then pick the papers out of the garbage and read them. Once, when Mandela picked up a newspaper lying on a bench, he was caught reading it and was punished. He had to stay in isolation and was deprived of meals. The sentences used to be for the smallest things, like giving a sidelong glance or failing to stand when a warder entered the room.

When prisoners asked for books, the authorities would be very careful not to give them anything of a political nature. Funnily enough, Little Red Riding Hood was rejected because it had the word Red in the title–Red was associated with the banned Communist Party. In 1978, after 15 years of agitation for the right to receive news, the authorities started their own 'radio news service'. This consisted of a daily summary of the news, read over the prison's intercom system. In 1980, finally the right to buy newspapers was granted. Soon they were also permitted to watch films and documentaries.

Whenever the prisoners wanted something to change, such as quality of food, they would go on a hunger strike. The hunger strikes were inspired by none other than our own Mahatma Gandhi. Other methods of protest were to observe go-slow strikes or refuse to clean up.

In 1969, Mandela was disturbed by the news that Winnie Mandela was arrested and charged with attempting to revive the ANC. In other words, she was an activist in the freedom struggle almost as much as Mandela was.

As the years passed, some of the rules were relaxed and the prisoners held competitions among themselves, organized a concert, put up a play and held birthday celebrations. Robben Island, at one point came to be known as the University. This was because knowledgeable prisoners like Mandela and Walter Sisulu would conduct lessons for other prisoners. Mandela spent a lot of time advising his fellow prisoners on legal matters.

Matters were not quiet in the outside world while Mandela was in prison. MK men were getting trained and indulged in sabotage and other disruptive acts. Many of them were caught and imprisoned in Robben Island.

On 16 June, 1976, 15,000 school children assembled in Soweto in Johannesburg and protested against the government's order that half of all classes in secondary schools must be taught in Afrikaans. Neither the students, nor the teachers wanted the language of the 'oppressor'. Police opened fire on the gathering of children, without warning. They killed a 13-year old boy Hector Pieterson and many others. Hundreds of children were wounded. The incident sparked off riots and violence across the country. Students boycotted schools and what was known as the 'Black Consciousness' movement sprang up among the youth.

In 1976, the Minister of Prisons, Jimmy Kruger, visited Mandela and offered that Mandela's sentence would be dramatically reduced if he was willing to move to Transkei, where he was born, and recognize the legitimacy of the government there. Mandela refused. In one more sign of improving conditions, in early 1977, the compulsory manual labour was stopped. Mandela used the extra time to pursue one of his favourite hobbies, gardening. He had asked for permission to grow a small garden for many years, but it was granted only in the 70s. He was soon providing the warders with tomatoes and onions.

A major step towards equality was taken in 1979 when the authorities announced that the diet for African, Coloured and Indian prisoners would be the same in future. Meanwhile, in South Africa and in other foreign countries, a 'Free Mandela' campaign was launched. Mandela became an international figure when he was awarded the Jawaharlal Nehru Human Rights Award in 1979. Naturally he could not go, and the head of the ANC, Oliver Tambo, received it on his behalf.

In 1982, Mandela was suddenly told to pack his things and that he was to be transferred out of the Island. Some of the senior ANC men in the prison were being transferred along with him. They were taken to the Pollsmoor maximum-security prison, a few miles from Cape Town. Mandela said that compared to Robben Island, 'we were in a five-star hotel'. Mandela, Walter Sisulu, Raymond Mhlaba and Andrew Mlangeni were put in a large room with a toilet, sinks, showers, beds, and towels. Luxury indeed!

Despite these amenities, Mandela felt isolated because he was cut off from his many comrades in Robben Island. Mandela cultivated a garden at Pollsmoor too. Using oil drums as containers, he grew onions, eggplants, cabbages, cauliflowers, beans, spinach, carrots, cucumbers, broccoli, beetroots, lettuce, tomatoes, peppers and strawberries. His 'farm' had nearly 900 plants. He supplied the vegetables to the prison kitchen. A welcome change came about in 1984 when he had a 'contact' visit from his family–in other words, they were no barriers between the prisoner and the visitors. They were also more aware of outside events thanks to newspapers and a radio. MK's attacks were increasing, a sign that the struggle was intensifying. In 1984, there was one more recognition for the anti-apartheid struggle, when Bishop Desmond Tutu was awarded the Nobel Peace Prize.

Negotiations

The government continued its efforts to win Mandela over. The countries President, P.W. Botha, during a debate in Parliament in 1985 offered Mandela his freedom if he 'unconditionally rejected violence as a political instrument'. Mandela responded by stating that he would not give any undertaking at a time when the people of South Africa were not free. His daughter read out his reply to a huge crowd of people in Johannesburg. Mandela said 'let Botha renounce violence, let him say that he will dismantle apartheid, let him unban the people's organization–The African National Congress!'

Nevertheless Mandela did initiate talks with the government in 1985, when he wrote to Minister of Justice Kobie Coetsee. They met later that year when

Mandela was hospitalised for prostate surgery. Shortly after this he was moved to a single cell at Pollsmoor .Mandela decided this was the right opportunity for him to confidentially begin the process of negotiations with the government.

At a meeting of the British Commonwealth in October 1985, the leaders could not agree on whether or not to participate in International sanctions against South Africa. To end the deadlock, the nations decided to send a delegation of eminent persons to South Africa on a fact-finding mission. Mandela met with the group in May that year. After making it clear that he was expressing his personal views, Mandela told them that many of the problems resulted from lack of communication between the government and the ANC. He asserted that violence would never be the final solution and suggested that if the Government withdrew the army and police from the townships, the ANC might agree to a suspension of the armed struggle. He made it clear that his release alone would not suffice.

When things were looking hopeful, the South African government launched air raids and commando attacks on ANC bases in Botswana, Zambia and Zimbabwe. This led to the eminent persons group immediately leaving South Africa. The attacks led to unrest and upheaval, and the government imposed emergency again to curb protest.

Mandela decided that negotiations could not wait and asked the commissioner of prisons, General Willemse to arrange a meeting between him and the Justice Minister. A series of tentative meetings took place, laying the groundwork for further contact and future negotiations, but little real progress was made.

There were other signs that the government was preparing him for a new life. One day, the deputy commander of Pollsmoor, took Mandela on a sightseeing trip of Cape Town. This happened several times. He was also taken to visit gardens where he could stroll, and to the beach. After initially feeling agitated, Mandela began enjoying these 'little adventures'.

In 1987, he contacted Coetsee again and had several private meetings with him. The minister said the government wanted to appoint a committee of senior officials to hold private talks with Mandela. This time Mandela consulted his fellow prisoners in Pollsmoor. They had some reservations but were on the whole not opposed to negotiations, and so began a series of meetings between Mandela and the government committee. He had to reassure them on several counts, for example whether minorities would be adversely affected by majority rule. He told them that 'no organization in South Africa could be compared with the ANC in attempts to unite all the peoples and races of the country'. He quoted from the Freedom Charter: 'South Africa belongs to all who live in it, black and white.'

In 1987, the ANC celebrated its 75th anniversary with a conference in Tanzania attended by delegates from over 50 nations. Earlier the same year, the National Party won yet another general election. Mandela came down with tuberculosis at this time. Fortunately it was an early stage of the ailment and he did not refrain from attending the meetings. Coetsee told Mandela that he wanted to put him in a condition halfway between confinement and freedom. Straight from hospital, he was taken to a one-story cottage set in the property of the Victor Verster Prison in the town of Paarl. This was about 35 miles from Cape Town. Mandela had a cook for himself, and living there gave him the illusion of freedom. After some time, some of his ANC comrades were permitted to visit him. The meetings with the committee continued and the issue of the ANC stopping violence repeatedly came up. Mandela would reply again and again that the state was the oppressor and was responsible for the violence. He wrote to President Botha with a framework for negotiations. Botha delayed and political violence and international pressure intensified. In 1989, some organizations got together to start a Mass Democratic Movement, which organized a defiance campaign of civil disobedience. This was also the time when Winnie Mandela was suspected of the murder of a young African. Mandela remained convinced of her innocence throughout.

In 1989, Mandela's 71st birthday was an occasion for almost his entire family to visit the cottage. That same month, he was suddenly told that he was being taken to see President Botha the following day. He prepared for the meeting with the man popularly knows as Die Groot Krokidil–the Great Crocodile. The meeting was more of a discussion about history and South African culture, than politics, but it was still a major step forward. Botha had suffered a stroke sometime earlier, and in August 1989 he resigned as President. The post was taken over by the head of the National Party, F W de Klerk. On the very day he was sworn in, Mandela wrote him a letter seeking a meeting. That de Klerk was different was soon evident when a march planned in Cape Town to protest police brutality was not banned. 'A new and different hand was on the tiller.'

Towards the end of the year, de Klerk announced that Walter Sisulu and seven of Mandela's former companions in Robben Island were to be released. de Klerk began an operation to end apartheid. He opened South African beaches to people of all colours and said that segregating regulations would soon be repealed. A meeting between Mandela and de Klerk took place on December 13, 1989. Mandela told de Klerk that the best way to move forward was to remove the ban on the ANC and other political organizations, lift emergency, release political prisoners and allow exiles to return. de Klerk was not a man to give immediate responses but he listened carefully to all that Mandela said. The meeting bore fruit on 2 February 1990, when de Klerk announced in parliament that the ban on ANC over 30 other organizations was being lifted, political prisoners in jail for non-violent activities would be freed, capital punishment suspended, and emergency restrictions lifted. 'The time for negotiation has arrived.' he said. Mandela and de Klerk met on 9 February and the President told him that he was going to be released. It had been, in all, 27 years in confinement.

Freedom

Mandela was released on 11 February, 1990. A huge crowd including journalists and television reporters had assembled at the gate of the prison. Mandela raised his right fist in the ANC salute, acknowledging the gathered crowd. It surprised him that many white families were standing by the road to get a glimpse of him. A much larger crowd was awaiting him in Cape Town where he was to address a rally. In his speech, he urged the people not to stop the campaign of mass action. He received congratulatory telegrams from Presidents and Prime Ministers of nations all over the world. The next day there was a press conference where he stressed that he might be out of jail, but he was not yet free. He and his wife flew to Johannesburg that evening. Mandela was told that thousands of people had surrounded his house, and that it would be unwise to go there. He stayed in the home of an ANC supporter instead.

The next day, hundred and twenty thousand people gathered at a stadium in Soweto. He gave a speech emphasizing that the crippling problems of urban African life had to be overcome, that students must return to school and that crime must be brought under control. Mandela once again embraced all the races and people of South Africa in his speech. That night and every night for the weeks and months after that, the house was surrounded by hundreds of people who sang and danced.

On February 27, he flew to Lusaka for a meeting of the ANC National Executive Committee. Several African heads of state were also present. At the session of the NEC, he was elected Deputy President of the ANC. Oliver Tambo was recovering from a stroke, so Alfred Nzo, the organization's Secretary General was named acting President. Mandela then went on a tour of Africa. He saw a world radically different from the one he had left. In Cairo, he told a press conference that the ANC was prepared 'to consider a cessation of hostilities'. He meant this as a signal to the South African government. Before he came back home, he flew to Stockholm to visit Oliver Tambo and then to London, to attend a concert held in his honour.

In March, a meeting with de Klerk was proposed, but there was a set back when on 26 March, police opened fire on ANC demonstrators killing twelve of them. Mandela announced a suspension of official talks. He met privately with de Klerk, however, and the date for negotiations was set as early May. The Afrikaan white government somehow wanted to keep some power for itself instead of giving it totally to the majority and this was the main hitch. Mandela described this as 'apartheid in disguise'. The talks took place in May, and at the end of the three-day meeting, both sides pledged to conduct peaceful negotiations and the government committed itself to lifting emergency. Mandela then made a personal visit to his hometown Qunu and paid homage at his mother's grave. She had died while he was still in prison.

Mandela then embarked on a tour of Europe and North America in June. A million people were present at his procession through New York. In Washington he addressed the U.S. Congress and thanked it for its anti-apartheid legislations.

Violence in South Africa was worsening at this time, and the death toll in the first six months of 1990 was over one thousand five hundred. Mandela felt that it was essential to speed up the normalization process but the government took a negative measure when it arrested forty senior ANC members claiming they were part of a plot to overthrow the government. Mandela told de Klerk that he had been misled. The ANC then took a step forward and voluntarily suspended the arms struggle.

Oliver Tambo returned to South Africa after three decades in exile. In July 1991, the ANC held its first annual conference inside South Africa in 30 years. Mandela was elected ANC President. The process of transforming of what had been an illegal underground liberation movement to a legal mass political party began. In the first 17 months of legal activity, the ANC recruited 700,000 members.

On 20 December 1991, the real talks began. They were called CODESA–the Convention for a Democratic South Africa. de Klerk then made the bold gesture of calling a nation-wide referendum of white people who would vote on his reform policy and on negotiations with the ANC. 69% of the white voters happily supported negotiation. de Klerk's hands were strengthened and negotiations continued.

Meanwhile, Mandela separated from his wife due to differences between them. He later married a third time.

Mandela and de Klerk jointly won the 1993 Nobel Peace Prize.

After some stumbling blocks and protest actions by ANC including a general strike, 3 June 1993 saw a major development. The multi-party forum voted to set a date for South Africa's national, non-racial, one-person-one-vote election on April 27, 1994. For the first time, the black majority would go to the polls to elect their own leaders.

ANC won the elections and Nelson Mandela became the first African President of South Africa.

www.ingramcontent.com/pod-product-compliance
Ingram Content Group UK Ltd.
Pitfield, Milton Keynes, MK11 3LW, UK
UKHW040003200726
13854UKWH00001B/17